# Income Shifting from Transfer Pricing:
# Further Evidence from Tax Return Data

by

## Michael McDonald*

## OTA Technical Working Paper 2
## July 2008

*OTA Technical Working Papers* is an occasional series of reports on the research, models and datasets developed to inform and improve Treasury's tax policy analysis. Views and opinions expressed are those of the authors and do not necessarily represent official Treasury positions or policy. *OTA Technical Working Papers* are distributed in order to document OTA analytic methods and data and invite discussion and suggestions for revision and improvement. Comments are welcome and should be directed to the authors.

Office of Tax Analysis
U.S. Department of the Treasury
1500 Pennsylvania Avenue, NW
Washington, D.C. 20220

* U.S. Department of the Treasury, Mike.McDonald@do.treas.gov

# Income shifting from Transfer Pricing:
## Further Evidence from Tax Return Data

## Abstract

*Abstract: The paper updates, modifies, and extends research by Grubert (2003) to investigate income shifting from intercompany transfer pricing. The analysis is based on theoretical and regression models developed in Grubert (2003). The models are modified slightly to capture the effects of "real" intercompany tangible, intangible, and services transactions (as opposed to interest 'income stripping' through intercompany or interbranch debt), and extended to incorporate data relating to cost sharing arrangements. Although some caution is required in interpreting the transfer pricing implications from the regression results, the empirical analysis generally supports concerns about potential non-arm's length income shifting under current transfer pricing rules.*

**Introduction: Income Shifting Under the Arm's Length Construct**

By definition, a multinational corporation conducts business and has an economic presence in more than one legal jurisdiction. Absent legal and tax considerations, territorial borders should not in themselves constitute barriers to the operations of the multinational group - notwithstanding that each of the associated enterprises of the multinational may be a legally distinct company in the jurisdictions in which it operates, the multinational maximizes worldwide profits by freely disseminating the sources of competitive advantage to members of the multinational group. In fact, any barriers to the effective exploitation of such competitive advantages would undermine the very rationale of the global operations of the multinational in the first place. "Transactions" between the associated enterprises involving tangible or intangible property, or the provision of services by one associated enterprise for another, are not market transactions, and therefore the pricing of such transactions – "transfer pricing" - is artificial and not in itself necessarily relevant to the maximization of global profits, since such internal transactions are zero-sum.[1]

Of course, territorial borders imply different legal environments and dual or even multiple taxing rights over the income of the multinational group. Accordingly, intercompany transactions may have tax implications. When multi-jurisdictional taxation is introduced, the taxing jurisdictions should have at least two taxing objectives. First, double taxation, or the imposition of tax by more than one jurisdiction on the same

---

[1] The artificiality of intercompany pricing of transactions is perhaps clearest in the case of a parent corporation with wholly-owned subsidiaries. However, even when ownership is less than total, if one corporation has effective control of associated enterprises, the transactions between the associated enterprises are still not market transactions; that is, transactions between independent entities.

income, should be avoided to the extent possible. Double taxation results in an impediment to cross border transactions and the movement of capital. Second, each taxing jurisdiction should tax an "appropriate" share of the profits of the multinational group. Determining such appropriate shares requires establishing prices on the transactions between the associated enterprises.

Many countries have agreed to a standard for determining transfer prices for tax purposes: the arm's-length principle. The arm's length principle and its relevance to the taxing rights of the jurisdictions is established in the Organisation for Economic Cooperation and Development (OECD) Model Tax Convention:

> [Where] conditions are made or imposed between the two [associated] enterprises in their commercial or financial relations which differ from those which would be made between independent enterprises, then any profits which would, but for those conditions, have accrued to one of the enterprises, but, by reason of those conditions, have not so accrued, may be included in the profits of that enterprise and taxed accordingly.[2] *(Bracketed words added for clarity).*

Fundamentally, the arm's length counterfactual is itself a construct, although a useful one that facilitates achievement of the two taxing objectives. With respect to the first objective, economic double taxation is eliminated in theory, and hopefully minimized in practice, through a taxing principle that can provide the basis for mutual agreement between taxing jurisdictions on how the taxing rights on intercompany transactions

---

[2] Article 9, paragraph 1 of the OECD Model Tax Convention on Income and on Capital. The United States uses identical language in the 2006 Model Income Tax Convention.

ultimately are determined or settled. For example, the OECD's Working Party No. 6 attempts to reach agreement on a myriad of technical transfer pricing issues in order to clarify the appropriate pricing of transactions. In doing so they also clarify (indirectly) the associated taxing rights in a way that minimizes double taxation relating to these intercompany transactions. The second objective – determining the "appropriate" taxing rights of each jurisdiction relating to the intercompany transactions – is inherently subjective. The arm's length principle attempts to simulate the working of markets. Simulating a market-based pricing system is intuitively appealing to economists, because the market's pricing mechanisms tend to result in an allocation of income commensurate with the economic contributions and competitive position of the respective participants.

The United States implements the arm's length principle through section 482 of the Internal Revenue Code and the associated regulations, which state in part:

> In determining the true taxable income of a controlled taxpayer, the standard to be applied in every case is that of a taxpayer dealing at arm's length with an uncontrolled taxpayer. A controlled transaction meets the arm's length standard if the results of the transaction are consistent with the results that would have been realized if uncontrolled taxpayers had engaged in the same transaction under the same circumstances (arm's length result). However, because identical transactions can rarely be located, whether a transaction produces an arm's length result generally will be determined by reference to the results of comparable transactions under comparable circumstances (see Treas. Reg. §1.482-1(d)(2) Standard of comparability). Evaluation of whether a controlled transaction

produces an arm's length result is made pursuant to a method selected under the best method rule. [3]

Unfortunately, attempting to determine arm's length pricing for transactions that are not arm's length, and perhaps would *not even take place* at arm's length, can be difficult in practice. The regulations recognize the difficult valuation issues involved, as reflected in the acceptance, in some circumstances, of a range of potential arm's length results rather than a single point; in the detailed guidance on the functional analysis, analysis of contractual terms, analysis of risk, and the analysis of economic conditions as an analytical roadmap for determining the arm's length counterfactual and its appropriate pricing; in the allowance of multiple year, rather than single year, analyses; and in the guidance on quantitative adjustments to enhance comparability and reliability.

While "arm's length" may be clear in concept, quantifying arm's length is a challenge. Transfers of intangible property can be particularly difficult to value in practice. Some intangibles, such as rights relating to important patents, software, or proprietary expertise, may be the *key* source of competitive advantage to a multinational corporation, and accordingly not typically transferred between unrelated parties (i.e., there are no comparable uncontrolled transactions). One type of arrangement relating to intangible property is worth noting here: cost sharing arrangements (CSAs). A CSA is an agreement between related parties to share in the costs of developing an intangible in proportion to each participant's share of anticipated benefits from the exploitation of the intangible to be developed. Under a CSA, each participant owns its appropriate share of

---

[3] Treas. Reg. §1.482-1(b) (1)

the developed intangible property, and consequently no licensing payments or other remuneration are required once the intangible property is developed. Because one or more parties may contribute intangibles at the outset of the CSA arrangement, the other CSA participants must provide arm's length remuneration for this contribution. This is called a "buy-in payment." While a CSA ultimately results in dual or multiple ownership of intangible property without the need for cross-licensing or other intercompany remuneration, this does *not* mean that CSAs are meant to be a vehicle for non-arm's length transfers of existing intangibles. In practice, it is the buy-in payment that ensures that CSAs are ultimately structured and priced at arm's length.

Particularly complex valuation issues arise under CSAs, in part from the structure of CSAs themselves. For example, the general section 482 guidance on valuing intangible property typically applies to existing (and thus currently exploitable) technology. In contrast, CSAs typically involve two different types of intangible property. The first type of intangible property is the *envisioned* (that is, not currently existing and therefore not currently exploitable) technology that is the very subject of the cost sharing arrangement. The second type of intangible property, the subject of the buy-in payment, is the existing intangible that is contributed by one or more of the cost sharing participants, whose value derives from the intangible's contribution *to the development of the envisioned intangible*, rather than, for example, to the contributed intangible's exploitation in its own right. Further, the second type of intangible property is often an "in-process" intangible that is not currently exploitable and therefore particularly difficult to value.

Thus, for intercompany transactions, and for transfers of intangible property in particular, valuation questions are often inherently difficult. This situation sometimes requires flexibility in determining appropriate valuation methods, which may invite broad ranges of "acceptable" arm's length outcomes. In the real world, when significantly different tax regimes (e.g., tax rates) across taxing jurisdictions and the flexibility under U.S. rules in repatriating foreign profits to the U.S. are also considered, policy makers understandably are concerned about companies' use of transfer pricing to shift income in order to achieve tax-advantaged results.

The opportunity to manipulate intercompany prices is a function of both the relative value of the transferred property to the taxpayer's business, and the difficulty in reliably pricing the transaction (which tends to support a wider range of practically "acceptable" arm's length prices). At one end of the spectrum, the intercompany transfers of commodities that are a relatively minor input to the production process pose little risk of income shifting: the value of the transferred property is small relative to the operations of the business, and there tend to be readily available reliable comparable transactions that define the arm's length price within a narrow, and not easily manipulable, range. On the other end of the spectrum, there is significant risk of income shifting from transfers of valuable intellectual property that are crucial to the core business of a taxpayer and that are difficult to value accurately.

By this standard, CSAs may pose a risk of income shifting from non-arm's length transfer pricing. In addition to the valuation and definitional problems discussed above,

CSAs often involve the key value-driving intangibles of a business. For example, it is not uncommon for CSAs to be for "future generations" of *all* products or licenses derived from the core technologies of a multinational group. With CSAs covering such a wide potential scope of activities, it is conceivable that multinational companies may effectively achieve the transfer of valuable intangibles to offshore locations for less than the full value required by U.S. law.[4]

This paper investigates whether there is evidence from tax return data of such income shifting. The paper updates, modifies, and extends prior research in the economics literature to investigate income shifting from intercompany transfer pricing. The analysis is based on theoretical and regression models developed in Grubert (2003). The model is modified slightly to capture the effects of "real" intercompany tangible, intangible, and services transactions (as opposed to interest "income stripping" through intercompany or interbranch debt), and extended to incorporate data relating to CSAs.

**Caveat Lector**

Some caution is required in assessing income shifting from transfer pricing using company-level data. Transfer pricing is intrinsically fact-dependent. Whether and the extent to which there may be income shifting from non-arm's length pricing of intercompany transactions sometimes can only be definitively determined at the very detailed level of the particular transactions under review, rather than at the level of a single company within a multinational group. There is some difficulty in drawing

---

[4] Specifically, section 367(d) requires remuneration for transfers of intangible property from U.S. taxpayers to foreign corporations, and section 482 of the Internal Revenue Code, and the associated 482 regulations establish methods for valuing transfers of intangible property for arm's length consideration.

inferences related strictly to transfer pricing solely from such aggregated data (that is, company-level data from hundreds or thousands of companies) for two reasons:

First, apparent income shifting in the aggregate data may in fact be fully supportable when specific transactions are analyzed. For example, it might be observed that the controlled foreign corporations (CFCs) of U.S.-based multinational corporations (MNCs) operating in low-tax jurisdictions have significantly higher profitability (measured relative to sales)[5] than the CFCs of these same U.S.-based MNCs operating in high-tax jurisdictions. For a particular multinational, however, this result may not necessarily be indicative of non-arm's length pricing of intercompany transactions. For example, a CFC operating in a low-tax jurisdiction may have developed a particular technology itself (for example through the independent efforts of its R&D activities) from which it earns above-normal returns, while a CFC in a high-tax jurisdiction may undertake only low-value routine activities that warrant relatively low profitability at arm's length (e.g., a similar level of profitability as that of unrelated companies undertaking similar functions and risks). Or MNCs may simply invest more in low-tax jurisdictions. The differential in profitability may be related to such differences in investment levels, as profitability tends to be related to capital intensity, all else being equal. As discussed below, the regression analysis used in this paper attempts to account for many of these factors. However, it would not be possible to isolate all of the factors other than transfer pricing that might explain the profitability patterns, so the implications of the regressions on income shifting from non-arm's length pricing are necessarily indirect.

---

[5] This measure of profitability is used throughout the paper. The rationale for using this measure is further discussed below.

Second, transfer pricing transactional detail may be "buried" within the broader financial data that are typically used for empirical analyses. There may be significant non-transfer pricing "noise" that hinders the ability to isolate transfer pricing effects, or to compare reliably the effects over time. For example, the "check-the-box" regulations issued in 1997 resulted in greater use of hybrid entities. One type of hybrid entity is an entity disregarded as separate from its owners according to U.S. tax rules, even though it may be a corporation under foreign law. Under tax consolidation rules, the hybrid "disappears" as its profit and loss results are rolled up into the consolidated return of the parent/affiliate. Importantly, what disappear are "zero sum" intercompany (which become interbranch) transactions. The years examined in this report are 1996 (prior to the 1997 check-the-box rules), 2000, and 2002.[6] Although the impact of the check-the-box rules bear most notably on intercompany interest payments (which this analysis explicitly eliminates from consideration in order to isolate, to the extent possible, other transfer pricing effects), the use of disregarded entities may itself further encourage non-arm's length pricing between foreign affiliates controlled by U.S. parents (see Altshuler and Grubert (2006) and Mutti and Grubert (2006)). Therefore, some caution is required in comparing 1996 and earlier years to 1997 and subsequent years. One reason is that under the filing rules of Form 5471, a CFC that checks the box to become a branch of other CFCs disappears from the tax file.[7] The "remaining" CFC may be in either a low-tax or high-tax jurisdiction. Another reason is that important transfer pricing regulatory

---

[6] 2002 and 2000 are the two most recent years of available data (components of the database are only compiled every other year). In addition, 1996 is included in order to benchmark the updated data to a prior analysis discussed below (Grubert(2003)).

[7] This issue would be particularly troublesome if the empirical analysis employed a "panel" data analysis; that is, an analysis that tracked particular CFCs over time.

developments also affected years subsequent to 1996, for example the §1.482-7 cost sharing regulations. Attempting to disentangle the transfer pricing effects that may be due to the check-the-box regulations from those that may be due specifically to the new cost sharing rules is difficult.

Notwithstanding the caveats discussed above, an examination of tax return data is useful in detecting and understanding patterns or relationships in the data that may point toward non-arm's length pricing or income shifting among related companies.

**A Brief Review of Recent Literature**

A number of studies have undertaken empirical investigations of income shifting. These can be categorized based on the data sources used: 1) aggregated, country-specific data; 2) firm-level data based on public (non-tax) filings of publicly traded companies, and 3) firm-level data based on tax and non-tax filings of U.S. multinationals and their CFCs.

In the first category, Grubert and Mutti (1991) use aggregated country-level BEA data on U.S. multinationals' affiliates to regress profit rates on local country statutory tax rates, while controlling for GDP growth, and conclude that the pattern of profitability in high- and low-tax jurisdictions is consistent with income shifting behavior. Hines and Rice (1994) use country-level aggregated data of non-bank CFCs (i.e., treating all foreign affiliates in a country as if owned by representative U.S. parent firms), and find evidence of sensitivity of profitability to local country effective tax rates, adjusting for financial structure and capital employed. Clausing (2001) uses aggregated country-level BEA data on intrafirm trade flows and shows that the intrafirm trade balance between the U.S. and its foreign affiliates, as well as intrafirm sales between foreign affiliates of U.S. MNCs, are related to effective tax rates in a manner consistent with, although not necessarily entirely explained by, income shifting.[8]

In the second category, Harris et al. (1993) use cross-sectional firm-level panel data from the public filings of 200 U.S. manufacturing corporations to investigate how differences in U.S. taxes as a percentage of U.S. sales or assets relate to subsidiary operations in foreign tax jurisdictions. Taking into account company characteristics (e.g., R&D and advertising as proxies for intangible assets, interest expense, and number of employees), and using indicators on the presence of an affiliate in a particular low-or high-tax jurisdiction, they show evidence of income shifting out of or into the United States consistent with (that is, negatively correlated with) tax rate differentials between the United States and foreign jurisdictions. Harris (1993) uses firm-level data from public filings of U.S. and foreign corporations to investigate the effects from major capital cost provisions in the Tax Reform Act of 1986 whose theoretical effect would unambiguously increase the incentive to shift income and/or capital to the United States from foreign affiliates independent of relative tax rates. Taking into account company characteristics pertaining to the level of "flexible" expenses (e.g., R&D, advertising, interest expense), and investigated separately from the U.S. and foreign perspective, he shows evidence that multinational companies shifted more income into the United States after the Tax Reform Act of 1986, and that they did so quickly. Jacob (1996) uses similar data to extend Harris (1993) by accounting for the volume of intercompany transactions between firms. His

---

[8] See also Keemsley "Comment" (2001).

12

analysis provides evidence that transfer pricing, rather than other factors, may explain the income shifting.

In the third category, Grubert and Slemrod (1998) use firm-level tax panel data of U.S. multinationals with subsidiaries in a particular low-tax jurisdiction (Puerto Rico), supplemented by data from public filings of the U.S. multinationals. They investigate, through probability regression models (probit, tobit) the joint investment and income shifting choices available to multinational firms, and find evidence that a large fraction of U.S. investment in Puerto Rico is due to the income shifting opportunities (uniquely) available there. Grubert (2003), of which this paper is an extension, seeks, in part, to address the somewhat limited applicability of Grubert and Slemrod (1998) by extending the analysis across a more comprehensive spectrum of low-tax and high-tax foreign jurisdictions. He uses firm-level tax data of U.S. CFCs, each matched to U.S. parent-level tax return data, and further supplemented with data from public filings of the U.S. parent. (A more detailed description of the data is provided below). The paper evaluates the correlation between pre-tax profitability and local country statutory tax rates, controlling for parent and CFC characteristics (e.g., CFC asset intensity, parent size, start-ups, and in particular the presence of intangible assets), and finds evidence of income shifting, primarily associated with industrial (rather than marketing) intangibles. The analysis is further extended to investigate and quantify the extent to which tax incentives to shift income increase the volume of related party transactions.

**Data**

13

The data used in this analysis are derived from the corporate tax return (Form 1120) file for each of the years, merged with information from Form 5471 (an information return filed for each of the U.S. parent's CFCs), and Form 1118 (by which a U.S. parent calculates its foreign tax credit for foreign taxes paid by its CFCs and branches). These tax return data were further matched, where possible, to financial data reported in public filings (e.g., SEC filings) of the U.S. parent. The sample is derived from the data for the 7,500 largest CFCs because detailed information is only available for them. The sample is further restricted by excluding financial CFCs and loss-making CFCs, and by applying other financial screens to eliminate significantly outlying observations.

**CFC Profitability in High- and Low-Tax Jurisdictions**

A CFC is defined in the Code as a foreign company, more than 50 percent of which is owned by "U.S. shareholders" (defined as U.S. persons, including entities, that own at least ten percent of the voting power of the company). If a multinational group is systematically engaging in non-arm's length pricing of intercompany transactions in order to facilitate purely tax-advantaged outcomes, we would expect to observe higher CFC profitability in low-tax jurisdictions and lower CFC profitability in high-tax jurisdictions, assuming other factors that affect profitability are equal. This section undertakes an investigation of CFC profitability based on tax return data for the years 1996, 2000, and 2002.

The incentives and mechanisms to shift income are available to U.S. corporations and their foreign affiliates, regardless of whether the transactions are between U.S. parents and their CFCs, or between foreign-controlled U.S. corporations and their parents, or between foreign affiliates of U.S. corporations. The tax data used in this paper happen to relate to U.S. corporations and their CFCs, but the results can be interpreted more broadly.

Figure 1 depicts the relationship between CFC profitability, measured by the ratio of operating profits to sales (or operating margin), and the statutory tax rate of the CFC jurisdiction.[9] Operating profits are defined as pre-tax earnings excluding interest income and interest expense, but including royalty income and royalty expense. The measure is based on "earnings and profits" (E&P), which are intended to approximate "book" operating profits. This measure of pre-tax operating profits has the advantage of being defined consistently across the taxing jurisdictions in which the CFCs operate. By excluding interest flows, the measure captures real ("above the line") activity, related to, for example, the flows of tangible, intangible, and services transactions between related and unrelated parties. Grubert (2003) discusses the rationale for using pre-tax, rather than post-tax, earnings to analyze potential income shifting. This operating margin measure has the further advantage of being a common "profit level indicator" when applying the comparable profits method under Treas. Reg. §1.482-5. Statutory tax rates are used rather than other measures (for example effective tax rates) because the shift of

---

[9] An alternative measure could be return on investment. For example, one measure of profitability could be operating profits divided by operating assets. However, assets are valued for book purposes based on historical value rather than at current market value. In addition, the reporting of asset data on tax forms is historically not as reliable as income data reported on tax forms. Notwithstanding these shortcomings, the analyses undertaken in this paper do incorporate by proxy a return to the contribution of assets by including asset intensity as a regressor. The approach therefore allows this important economic contributor to CFC profitability to be taken into account, albeit imperfectly, so that ultimately the tax effects can be more reliably measured.

an additional dollar of income from one taxing jurisdiction to another would result in a change in tax equal to the difference in the marginal tax rates of the jurisdictions. The marginal tax rate is best captured by the jurisdiction's statutory tax rate.

Figure 1 depicts the relationship between operating margin and tax rates for all non-financial CFCs for each of the tax years analyzed. In general, the curves slope downward (although certainly not monotonically, notably in 1996), indicating an inverse relationship between pre-tax profitability and tax rates. For example, in 2002 the weighted average pre-tax operating margins were over 20 percent for CFCs operating in tax jurisdictions with a zero percent statutory tax rate, while the pre-tax operating margins were under 8 percent for CFCs operating in tax jurisdictions with statutory tax rates over 35 percent.

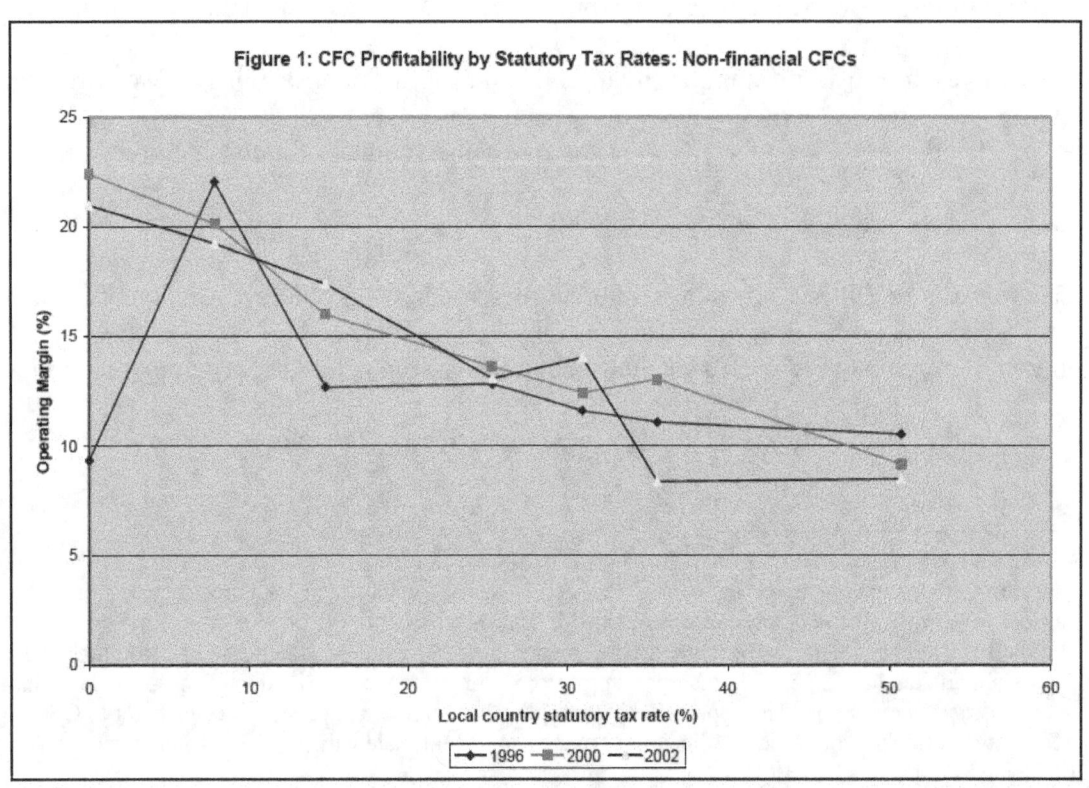

In order to more carefully examine the relationship between CFC profitability and local country tax rates - in particular to capture as many of the non-transfer pricing factors as possible – a regression analysis is undertaken.

**Regression Analysis**

The regression analyses presented in Tables 1 through 4 are based on the model presented in Grubert (2003), updated through 2002 and supplemented to incorporate new transfer pricing-specific data. The dependent variable in the Table 1 regressions is the ratio of CFC pre-tax operating profits to CFC sales (that is, the dependent variable is the operating margin depicted in Figure 1). As discussed above, the dependent variable in these regressions is slightly different than the dependent variable in Grubert (2003), as Grubert's income measure *includes* interest income and interest expense, and the analysis here excludes interest flows. As in Grubert (2003), a negative correlation between operating margins and the statutory tax rate, controlling for the other non-tax factors (which should have an independent effect on profitability), can be interpreted as providing evidence of possible income shifting through transfer pricing.

| Table 1:  Non-Financial CFC Profitability | | | | |
|---|---|---|---|---|
| Dependent Variable:  Ratio of CFC operating profit to sales (T-statistics in parentheses) | | | | |
| | | **1996** | **2000** | **2002** |
| **Independent Variables:** | | | | |
| Intercept | | .083 (2.69) | .115 (5.22) | .129 (5.76) |
| CFC Age < 5 years | | .024 (2.74) | .02 (1.82) | -.01 (-1.21) |
| CFC Age 5-15 years | | .015 (2.42) | .029 (3.99) | .02 (2.89) |

| | | | | |
|---|---|---|---|---|
| Parent R&D / Sales | | .224 (1.28) | .406 (3.48) | .219 (1.86) |
| Parent Advertising / Sales | | .112 (1.28) | .093 (0.8) | .06 (0.44) |
| Parent domestic profits / sales | | -.01 (-1.7) | .0001 (1.09) | -.0001 (-.69) |
| **Local statutory tax rate** | | **-.109 (-4.6)** | **-.17 (-6.23)** | **-.216 (-6.98)** |
| Log of parent sales | | .002 (1.02) | .001 (0.39) | .003 (1.49) |
| CFC assets / sales | | .045 (20.93) | .045 (22.96) | .033 (16.92) |
| | | | | |
| Adjusted R2 | | .1779 | .2354 | .1574 |
| | | | | |
| Mean of dependent variable | | .1445 | .1645 | .1585 |
| | | | | |
| Number of observations | | 2,290 | 2,047 | 1,953 |

Turning to the non-tax factors in table 1, asset intensity (the regressor CFC assets / sales) not surprisingly had a positive and statistically very significant effect on profitability for all years. CFCs that were between five and fifteen years old also were statistically more profitable than older CFCs in all three years. Start-up CFCs (that is, CFCs under 5 years) were also more profitable than older CFCs in 1996 and 2000. Although this would be a surprising result for pure start-up CFCs, the data would also reflect mergers. Parent R&D intensity, a proxy for CFCs in intellectual property-intensive industries, not surprisingly had a positive and generally significant effect on profitability for all three years.[10] The proxies for parent size (log of parent sales), parent advertising intensity, and parent profitability (parent domestic profits / sales) had an effect on CFC profitability that was generally not statistically significant, although generally with the expected sign.

---

[10] The coefficient was positive and significant at the 1 percent level and 7 percent level in 2000 and 2002, respectively and was positive, but only significant at the 20 percent level in 1996.

Turning to the tax related factor, Table 1 shows that, even when important non-tax factors are accounted for, higher local country statutory tax rates had a negative and statistically significant effect on the operating margin of CFCs. In fact, the coefficient increases significantly between 1996 and 2002, indicating a widening of the profitability disparities between high- and low-tax jurisdictions over that time. As discussed above, some caution is required in comparing 1996 to subsequent years. While the results nominally support income shifting that is increasing over time, this may not necessarily be the case. For example, to the extent that "surviving" CFCs after checking-the-box reside in low-tax jurisdictions, the income could be higher between 1996 and 2000 for reasons other than pricing manipulation. Of course, surviving CFCs could also be in high-tax jurisdictions, so the net effect is ambiguous. Also, note that the statutory tax rate parameter *does* become more negative between 2000 and 2002. The check-the-box rules were obviously applicable for both of these years, and so is not a differentiating factor.

It is important to recall again that these results do not in themselves necessarily point to transfer pricing abuse as the underlying cause of the inverse relationship between tax rates and profitability. The data are aggregated beyond the transactional level necessary for such a determination, and in addition there were no transfer pricing specific regressors to evaluate. Nevertheless, because the analysis takes into account many non-transfer pricing economic factors that could affect profitability, the hypothesis that multinationals engage in non arm's length pricing of intercompany transactions in order to facilitate purely tax-advantaged outcomes clearly cannot be rejected by the available data – in both

19

the pre- and post- check-the-box years. This result is consistent with the existing economics literature.

As discussed above, information directly relevant to transfer pricing is not typically contained in the aggregated financial accounts of multinational corporations, nor is a clear trail of evidence relating to transfer pricing found on tax return information filed by multinationals, including Form 5471. In view of the limitations of the available data, it is only possible to draw transfer pricing inferences by ruling out as many non-transfer pricing factors as possible, as illustrated in Table 1.

In order to address these data limitations, the IRS was asked in 2006 to undertake a survey of its International Examiners and economists in order to identify the multinational corporations that have in the past engaged in cost sharing arrangements (CSAs) or are currently engaged in CSAs with any of their CFCs. The survey information included the names of U.S. parent companies that have at least one CSA, the starting year of the CSAs identified, the names of the CFCs participating in the CSAs, and some information on audit activity of the CSAs. The survey does not include any detailed information on the CSAs themselves, such as the type of cost shared intangibles, the buy-in payments, or any financial information specifically associated with the CSAs. The survey cannot be considered comprehensive (that is, as capturing all CSAs) and, given the methodology, should be considered more reliable for more recent, rather than more distant, years. Nevertheless, such information might be useful in broadly assessing profitability across taxing jurisdictions comparing the CFCs of U.S. multinationals engaging in CSAs with one or more of their CFCs with CFCs of U.S. multinationals not engaging in CSAs.

Although these data allow the analysis to move a step closer towards the investigation of income shifting through specific transfer pricing transactions, the results of this analysis are not determinative, and should again be interpreted with some caution. The data identify U.S. parents that undertake CSAs, but the data do not provide the level of transactional detail necessary to make a more targeted assessment of CSAs under the Treas. Reg. §1.482-7 regulations, or to determine the extent to which the results are driven by the CSAs themselves. More work is needed to refine the analysis further.

The regression model presented in Table 2 contains the same explanatory variables as in Table 1, but adds two explanatory variables related to CSAs. The first is a dummy variable that identifies all CFCs whose U.S. parent has been identified as engaging in CSAs.[11] Note that this definition captures CFCs that may not themselves be explicit participants with their parent company in the CSAs. Including these non-participating CFCs is appropriate, since the effects of CSAs would typically impact the financial results of CFCs beyond those that are engaged in the legal arrangement. For example, a CFC that is a CSA participant may license the developed intangible to affiliated CFCs that are not themselves participants in the CSA, but whose financial results are

---

[11] For a given year, the dummy variable is '1' only if the U.S. parent has been identified as having CSAs whose starting date predates the end of that tax year. For example, a parent whose CSA commences in 1999 will be assigned a dummy of '0' for 1996, and '1' for 2000 and 2002. As discussed above, the "non-CSA" control group is not a perfect measure, as it is theoretically possible that some parents involved in CSAs were not identified in the survey. However, given the fact that the data are comprised of only the largest CFCs, the potential under-identification is not likely to be significant.

nevertheless impacted by the CSA through the licensing or other payments they make. The second explanatory variable is the product of the local country statutory rate and the CSA dummy variable. This variable captures the incremental effect of the relationship between pre-tax profitability and tax rates for those CFCs whose parents engage in CSAs. The relationship between pre-tax operating profit and local country tax rates for CFCs of parents engaged in CSAs can be determined by summing the coefficient for "local statutory tax rate" and the coefficient for "local statutory tax rate times parent cost sharing status".

| Table 2: Non-Financial CFC Profitability Including Cost Sharing Effects<br>Dependent Variable: Ratio of CFC operating profit to sales<br>T-statistic in parentheses | | | |
|---|---|---|---|
| | **1996** | **2000** | **2002** |
| **Independent Variables:** | | | |
| Intercept | .08<br>(2.49) | .12<br>(5.42) | .127<br>(5.52) |
| **Parent cost sharing status** | **.09**<br>**(3.01)** | **.02**<br>**(0.56)** | **.045**<br>**(1.79)** |
| CFC Age < 5 years | .02<br>(2.66) | .016<br>(1.84) | -.011<br>(-1.22) |
| CFC Age 5-15 years | .015<br>(2.49) | .029<br>(3.95) | .022<br>(2.97) |
| Parent R&D / Sales | .232<br>(1.33) | .39<br>(3.36) | .201<br>(1.68) |
| Parent Advertising / Sales | .106<br>(1.21) | .08<br>(0.72) | .063<br>(0.49) |
| Parent domestic profits / sales | -.005<br>(-1.73) | .0001<br>(1.15) | -.0001<br>(-.6) |
| **Local statutory tax rate** | **-.086**<br>**(-3.44)** | **-.17**<br>**(-5.82)** | **-.193**<br>**(-5.59)** |
| **LS tax rate * parent cost sharing status** | **-.223**<br>**(-2.88)** | **.008**<br>**(0.1)** | **-.116**<br>**(-1.5)** |
| Log of parent sales | .002<br>(0.82) | -.0001<br>(-0.06) | .002<br>(1.1) |
| CFC assets / sales | .045<br>(20.98) | .046<br>(22.8) | .033<br>(16.8) |
| | | | |
| Adjusted R2 | .1840 | .236 | .1623 |
| | | | |
| Mean of dependent variable | .1445 | .1645 | .1585 |
| Number of observations associated w/ CSAs | 201 | 263 | 343 |
| Number of observations | 2,290 | 2,047 | 1,953 |

Turning first to the most recent year, 2002, CFCs whose parents engage in CSAs tend to be more profitable in general than other CFCs, with significance at the 7 percent level. In addition, the coefficient on the CSA-tax rate variable has the expected sign (that is, these CFCs have higher profitability in low-tax jurisdictions and lower profitability in high-tax jurisdictions than their non-CSA cohorts), but the coefficient is not statistically different from zero at traditional confidence levels.[12]

In the year 2000 analysis, the CSA-related tax coefficient is not statistically different from zero, indicating that multinationals engaging in CSAs do not exhibit more pronounced income shifting than the non-CSA cohort in that year.

The results for 1996 are notable for two reasons. First, the CFCs associated with these multinational parents were significantly more profitable and had a significantly more negative correlation between pre-tax profits and local country tax rates than the non-CSA cohort, even when the non-tax factors affecting profitability are taken into account. Second, cost sharing arrangements prior to 1996 would correspond to CSA rules that pre-date the current Treas. Reg. §1.482-7 regulations.[13]

---

[12] The coefficient is significant at the 13 percent level. One factor not explicitly accounted for in this analysis is the possible influence of CSAs that are in early, unprofitable stages. This is addressed below.

[13] The guidance provided in the regulations, effective for years 1968 through 1995, consisted of a single paragraph, which read, "Where a member of a group of controlled entities acquires an interest in intangible property as a participating party in a bona fide cost sharing arrangement with respect to the development of such intangible property, the district director shall not make allocations with respect to such acquisition except as may be appropriate to reflect each participant's arm's length share of the costs and risks of developing the property. A bona fide cost sharing arrangement is an agreement, in writing, between two or more members of a group of controlled entities providing for the sharing of the costs and risks of developing intangible property in return for a specified interest in the intangible property that may be produced. In order for the arrangement to qualify as a bona fide arrangement, it must reflect an effort in good faith by the participating members to bear their respective shares of all the costs and risks of development on an arm's length basis. In order for the sharing of costs and risks to be considered on an arm's length basis, the terms and conditions must be comparable to those which would have been adopted by unrelated parties similarly situated had they entered into such an arrangement. If an oral cost sharing arrangement, entered into prior to April 16, 1968, and continued in effect after that date, is otherwise in compliance with the standards prescribed in this subparagraph, it shall constitute a bona fide cost sharing arrangement if it is reduced to writing prior to January 1, 1969." See Treas. Reg. §1.482-2A(d)(4).

To summarize, based on the results presented in Table 2, the evidence that CSAs have provided a possible means for more pronounced income shifting is somewhat mixed. However, the analysis above does not account for what might be called post-1996 "CSA vintaging" effects: Because the CSA regulations were substantially revised in 1996, it is possible that the data for a number of years after 1996 (possibly even as late as 2002) incorporate CSAs in their early stages. Since a CSA is an agreement to share costs – typically early-year research costs and buy-in payments – in order to exploit *future* envisioned intangibles, it would not be surprising for a CSA to experience operating losses in early years and operating gains (to the extent that the CSA is ultimately successful) only in later years. Accordingly, in those early years, the relationship between CFC profitability and statutory tax rates would tend to be *positive*, rather than negative, even for those CSAs that *ultimately* produce non-arm's length income shifting. Thus, in order to more carefully assess the effects of the current Treas. Reg. §1.482-7 cost sharing regulations on the data, some adjustment for this CSA vintaging effect is warranted.

Tables 3 and 4 summarize the results from adjusting for CSA vintaging for 2002 and 2000, respectively. In Table 3, the first column of results reproduces the results in Table 2 for 2002, that is, a CFC is considered to be associated with CSAs if its parent has CSAs with starting dates in any year prior to the end of 2002. In the second column of results, a CFC is considered to be associated with CSAs only if its parent has CSAs with starting dates prior to the end of 1999. Thus, only CSAs that are at least three years old are incorporated into the CSA dummy variables. In the third column of results, a CFC is considered to be associated with a CSA only if its parent has CSAs with starting dates prior to the end of 1996. Thus, only CSAs that are at least six years old are incorporated into the CSA dummy variables.

| Table 3: 2002 Non-Financial CFC Profitability Including Cost Sharing Effects Dependent Variable: Ratio of 2002 CFC operating profit to sales T-statistic in parentheses | | | |
|---|---|---|---|
| | CSAs prior to 2003 | CSA's prior to 2000 | CSAs prior to 1997 |
| **Independent Variables:** | | | |
| Intercept | .127 (5.52) | .126 (5.46) | .133 (5.78) |
| **Parent cost sharing status** | **.045 (1.8)** | **.051 (1.81)** | **.087 (2.63)** |
| CFC Age < 5 years | -.011 (-1.22) | -.01 (-1.18) | -.01 (-1.17) |
| CFC Age 5-15 years | .022 (2.97) | .022 (2.96) | .022 (2.94) |
| Parent R&D / Sales | .201 (1.68) | .216 (1.82) | .231 (1.95) |
| Parent Advertising / Sales | .063 (0.49) | .062 (0.48) | .051 (.40) |
| Parent domestic profits / sales | -.0001 (-.6) | -.0001 (-.6) | -.0001 (-.55) |
| **Local statutory tax rate** | **-.193 (-5.59)** | **-.193 (-5.77)** | **-.193 (-5.92)** |
| **LS tax rate * parent cost sharing status** | **-.116 (-1.5)** | **-.147 (-1.71)** | **-.213 (-2.11)** |
| Log of parent sales | .002 (1.1) | .002 (1.2) | .002 (0.78) |
| CFC assets / sales | .033 (16.8) | .033 (16.8) | .033 (16.9) |
| | | | |
| Adjusted R2 | .1623 | .158 | .16 |
| Mean of dependent variable | .1585 | .1585 | .1585 |
| Number of observations associated w/ CSAs | 343 | 292 | 203 |
| Number of observations | 1953 | 1953 | 1953 |

The results in Table 3 indicate that, when CSA vintaging is taken into account, CFCs associated with CSAs have higher profitability in low-tax jurisdictions and lower profitability in high-tax jurisdictions than their non-CSA cohorts, at statistically significant levels. The older the "vintage" of the CSAs, the more pronounced are the effects, both in magnitude and in significance. Thus, the data provide more evidence of incremental income shifting associated with CSAs than the model presented in Table 2.

| Table 4: 2000 Non-Financial CFC Profitability Including Cost Sharing Effects Dependent Variable: Ratio of 2000 CFC operating profit to sales T-statistic in parentheses | | | | |
|---|---|---|---|---|
| | | CSAs prior to 2001 | CSA's prior to 1996 | CSAs prior to 1994 |
| **Independent Variables:** | | | | |
| Intercept | | .12 (5.42) | .12 (5.51) | .12 (5.49) |
| **Parent cost sharing status** | | **.02 (0.56)** | **.03 (0.9)** | **.06 (1.81)** |
| CFC Age < 5 years | | .016 (1.84) | .016 (1.86) | .016 (1.8) |
| CFC Age 5-15 years | | .029 (3.95) | .029 (3.94) | .029 (3.95) |
| Parent R&D / Sales | | .39 (3.36) | .40 (3.45) | .40 (3.43) |
| Parent Advertising / Sales | | .08 (0.72) | .08 (0.65) | .08 (0.71) |
| Parent domestic profits / sales | | .0001 (1.15) | .0001 (1.17) | .0001 (1.19) |
| **Local statutory tax rate** | | **-.17 (-5.82)** | **-.17 (-5.86)** | **-.16 (-5.64)** |
| **LS tax rate * parent cost sharing status** | | **.008 (0.1)** | **-.002 (-.03)** | **-.08 (-.89)** |
| Log of parent sales | | -.0001 (-0.06) | -.0001 (-.19) | -.0001 (-.29) |
| CFC assets / sales | | .046 (22.8) | .045 (22.8) | .045 (22.72) |
| | | | | |
| Adjusted R2 | | .236 | .237 | .237 |
| | | | | |
| Mean of dependent variable | | .1645 | .1645 | .1645 |
| | | | | |
| Number of observations associated w/ CSAs | | 263 | 187 | 164 |
| Number of observations | | 2,047 | 2,047 | 2,047 |

The results in Table 4 similarly show that, as in Table 2, the coefficients have the expected sign, but the results are not statistically different than zero.

The regression analyses summarized in Tables 1 through 4 were also run on a CFC sales-weighted basis, as shown in Tables 5 through 8. The sales-weighted regressions provide further insights into the more aggregated effects of potential CFC income shifting, as well as further adjustment for CFC size compared with the unweighted regressions.

As in the unweighted regressions, the weighted regressions show significantly higher profitability in low-tax jurisdictions and lower profitability in high-tax jurisdictions, providing evidence of possible income shifting. The tax coefficients in Table 5 are similar in magnitude and significance to the tax coefficients in Table 1.

With respect to the effects of cost sharing arrangements, the evidence from the weighted analysis– similar to the unweighted analysis – is somewhat mixed. As shown in Table 6, the CSA-related tax coefficient is not as pronounced or as significant in 1996 as in the unweighted regression (Table 2) - the CSA tax coefficient is significant at the eight percent level. For 2000, CFCs whose parents engage in CSAs were not statistically different than other CFCs. However, for 2002 the CSA-related tax coefficient shown in Table 6 is both more pronounced and more significant (at the one percent level) than in the unweighted regression.

With respect to accounting for CSA vintaging effects, Table 7 shows even more pronounced and significant results in 2002 for CSAs undertaken prior to 2000 than in the unweighted analysis. However, for CSAs undertaken prior to 1996 – corresponding to CSAs undertaken prior to the revised 1996 cost sharing regulations – the CSA tax coefficient is not statistically significant. With respect to 2000, Table 8 shows no evidence of incremental potential income shifting effects for CFCs associated with CSAs when vintaging is taken into account.

Taken altogether, the results from the weighted and unweighted analyses show that the data are not inconsistent with the existence of possible income shifting. In addition, the analyses provide evidence – although not indisputable evidence – that CFCs whose parents participate in CSAs may engage in more aggressive income shifting.

## Table 5: Non-Financial CFC Profitability
Dependent Variable: Ratio of CFC operating profit to sales
(T-statistics in parentheses)
Weighted by CFC Sales

| | | 1996 | 2000 | 2002 |
|---|---|---|---|---|
| **Independent Variables:** | | | | |
| Intercept | | .121 (3.92) | .111 (5.32) | .097 (4.44) |
| CFC Age < 5 years | | .002 (0.2) | .008 (1.08) | -.01 (-2.12) |
| CFC Age 5-15 years | | -.003 (-.48) | -.002 (-0.04) | .02 (2.67) |
| Parent R&D / Sales | | .067 (0.41) | .551 (5.52) | .474 (4.6) |
| Parent Advertising / Sales | | .205 (2.35) | .198 (1.81) | .905 (7.54) |
| Parent domestic profits / sales | | .001 (0.1) | .0001 (1.15) | -.0001 (-.86) |
| **Local statutory tax rate** | | **-.110 (-5.27)** | **-.202 (-8.33)** | **-.206 (-7.2)** |
| Log of parent sales | | -.002 (-1.29) | .001 (0.25) | .002 (0.11) |
| CFC assets / sales | | .072 (23.62) | .055 (24.25) | .043 (19.27) |
| | | | | |
| Adjusted R2 | | .2091 | .2714 | .2496 |
| | | | | |
| Mean of dependent variable | | .1175 | .1318 | .1246 |
| | | | | |
| Number of observations | | 2,290 | 2,047 | 1,953 |

## Table 6: Non-Financial CFC Profitability Including Cost Sharing Effects
### Dependent Variable: Ratio of CFC operating profit to sales
T-statistic in parentheses
Weighted by CFC Sales

| | | 1996 | 2000 | 2002 |
|---|---|---|---|---|
| **Independent Variables:** | | | | |
| Intercept | | .123 (3.86) | .115 (5.31) | .08 (3.59) |
| **Parent cost sharing status** | | **.047 (1.85)** | **-.017 (-0.83)** | **.062 (3.05)** |
| CFC Age < 5 years | | .002 (0.18) | .009 (1.11) | -.02 (-2.62) |
| CFC Age 5-15 years | | -.002 (-0.42) | -.0003 (-.06) | .020 (2.79) |
| Parent R&D / Sales | | .072 (0.44) | .544 (5.44) | .476 (4.56) |
| Parent Advertising / Sales | | .198 (2.26) | .195 (1.75) | .89 (7.43) |
| Parent domestic profits / sales | | .005 (0.1) | .0001 (1.15) | -.0001 (-.9) |
| **Local statutory tax rate** | | **-.097 (-4.45)** | **-.22 (-7.97)** | **-.149 (-4.49)** |
| **LS tax rate * parent cost sharing status** | | **-.123 (-1.75)** | **.05 (0.94)** | **-.206 (-3.31)** |
| Log of parent sales | | -.002 (-1.44) | .0004 (0.21) | .002 (0.12) |
| CFC assets / sales | | .073 (23.55) | .056 (24.15) | .043 (19.49) |
| | | | | |
| Adjusted R2 | | .2096 | .271 | .2531 |
| | | | | |
| Mean of dependent variable | | .1175 | .1318 | .1246 |
| Number of observations associated w/ CSAs | | 201 | 263 | 343 |
| Number of observations | | 2,290 | 2,047 | 1,953 |

| | | CSAs prior to 2003 | CSA's prior to 2000 | CSAs prior to 1997 |
|---|---|---|---|---|
| **Table 7: 2002 Non-Financial CFC Profitability Including Cost Sharing Effects** Dependent Variable: Ratio of 2002 CFC operating profit to sales T-statistic in parentheses Weighted by CFC Sales | | | | |
| **Independent Variables:** | | | | |
| Intercept | | .08 (3.59) | .08 (3.45) | .09 (4.23) |
| **Parent cost sharing status** | | **.062 (3.05)** | **.077 (3.58)** | **.021 (0.82)** |
| CFC Age < 5 years | | -.02 (-2.62) | -.02 (-2.48) | -.01 (-2.15) |
| CFC Age 5-15 years | | .020 (2.79) | .02 (2.81) | .02 (2.69) |
| Parent R&D / Sales | | .476 (4.56) | .491 (4.73) | .481 (4.65) |
| Parent Advertising / Sales | | .89 (7.43) | .916 (7.64) | .91 (7.44) |
| Parent domestic profits / sales | | -.0001 (-.9) | -.0001 (-.94) | -.0001 (-.86) |
| **Local statutory tax rate** | | **-.149 (-4.49)** | **-.146 (-4.5)** | **-.196 (-6.33)** |
| **LS tax rate * parent cost sharing status** | | **-.206 (-3.31)** | **-.256 (-3.86)** | **-.07 (-0.86)** |
| Log of parent sales | | .002 (0.12) | .002 (0.17) | .002 (0.08) |
| CFC assets / sales | | .043 (19.49) | .043 (19.58) | .043 (19.27) |
| | | | | |
| Adjusted R2 | | .2531 | .2546 | .2491 |
| Mean of dependent variable | | .1246 | .1246 | .1246 |
| Number of observations associated w/ CSAs | | 343 | 292 | 203 |
| Number of observations | | 1,953 | 1,953 | 1,953 |

| | | CSAs prior to 2001 | CSA's prior to 1996 | CSAs prior to 1994 |
|---|---|---|---|---|
| **Table 8:  2000 Non-Financial CFC Profitability Including Cost Sharing Effects** Dependent Variable:  Ratio of 2000 CFC operating profit to sales T-statistic in parentheses Weighted by CFC Sales | | | | |
| **Independent Variables:** | | | | |
| Intercept | | .115 (5.31) | .122 (5.69) | .118 (5.48) |
| **Parent cost sharing status** | | **-.017 (-0.83)** | **-.01 (-.37)** | **.003 (0.13)** |
| CFC Age < 5 years | | .009 (1.11) | .009 (1.17) | .008 (1.1) |
| CFC Age 5-15 years | | -.0003 (-.06) | -.0003 (-.08) | -.0002 (-.03) |
| Parent R&D / Sales | | .544 (5.44) | .547 (5.48) | .547 (5.48) |
| Parent Advertising / Sales | | .195 (1.75) | .15 (1.32) | .167 (1.49) |
| Parent domestic profits / sales | | .0001 (1.15) | .0001 (1.20) | .0001 (1.19) |
| **Local statutory tax rate** | | **-.22 (-7.97)** | **-.21 (-8.16)** | **-.204 (-7.94)** |
| **LS tax rate * parent cost sharing status** | | **.05 (0.94)** | **.08 (1.15)** | **0.2 (0.39)** |
| Log of parent sales | | .0004 (0.21) | -.0004 (-.21) | -.0002 (-.11) |
| CFC assets / sales | | .056 (24.15) | .055 (23.84) | .055 (23.87) |
| | | | | |
| Adjusted R2 | | .271 | .272 | .2711 |
| | | | | |
| Mean of dependent variable | | .1318 | .1318 | .1318 |
| Number of observations associated w/ CSAs | | 263 | 187 | 164 |
| Number of observations | | 2,047 | 2,047 | 2,047 |

## Conclusion

The arm's length principle has proven its value as an effective tool in minimizing economic double taxation and in ultimately clarifying taxing rights associated with intercompany transfers. Nevertheless, the "arm's length construct" can be difficult to evaluate, especially for transfers of valuable intangible property. The transfer of intangible property associated with cost sharing arrangements, especially buy-in payments, has proven particularly difficult to price appropriately. For these reasons, and based on the experience of the IRS in administering the transfer pricing rules, policymakers have expressed some concern that transfer pricing can be a tool to shift income inappropriately. This paper extends prior economic research to investigate whether tax return data of CFCs are consistent with income shifting. The paper modifies and updates Grubert (2003), and extends the empirical work to incorporate information on CSAs. While the ability to draw transactional transfer pricing inferences from tax return and CSA data is to some extent limited, the analysis demonstrates that the tax data are consistent with (although do not conclusively prove) the existence of potential income shifting from non-arm's length transfer pricing.

# References

Altshuler, Rosanne, and Harry Grubert (2006), "The Three Parties in the Race to the Bottom: Host Countries, Home Countries, and Multinational Companies," *Tax Notes*, February 27, 2006, pp. 979-992.

Clausing, Kimberly A. (2001), "The impact of Transfer Pricing on Intrafirm Trade," in International Taxation and Multinational Activity, edited by James R. Hines, Jr., 173-194.

Clausing, Kimberly A. (2006), "International Tax Avoidance and U.S. International Trade," *National Tax Journal* 59(2), June 2006, pp. 269-287.

Grubert, Harry and John Mutti (1991), "Taxes, Tariffs and Transfer pricing in Multinational Corporation Decision Making," *Review of Economics and Statistics* 33: 285-293.

Grubert, Harry and John Mutti (2006), "New Developments in the Effect of Taxes on Royalties and the Migration of Intangible Assets Abroad," *NBER Working Paper*.

Grubert, Harry (2003), "Intangible Income, Intercompany Transactions, Income Shifting and the Choice of Location," *National Tax Journal* 56(1) part 2, March 2003, pp. 221-242.

Grubert, Harry and Joel Slemrod (1998), "The Effect of Taxes on Investment and Income Shifting to Puerto Rico," *Review of Economics and Statistics* 80: 365-373.

Harris, David, Randall Morck, Joel Slemrod, and Bernard Yeung (1993), "Income Shifting in U.S. Multinational Corporations," in Alberto Giovannini, R. Glenn Hubbard, and Joel Slemrod (eds.), Studies in International Taxation (Chicago: University of Chicago Press).

Harris, David G. (1993), "The Impact of U.S. Tax Law Revision on Multinational Corporations' Capital Location and Income-Shifting Decisions," *Journal of Accounting Research* 31: pp. 111-140.

Hines, James R., Jr., and Eric Rice (1994), "Fiscal Paradise: Foreign Tax Havens and American Business," *Quarterly Journal of Economics*, 109: (February) pp. 149-182.

Jacob, John (1996), "Taxes and Transfer Pricing: Income Shifting and the Volume of Intrafirm Transfers," *Journal of Accounting Research* 34, pp. 301-312.

Kemsley, Deen (2001) "Comment on 'The impact of Transfer Pricing on Intrafirm Trade'," in International Taxation and Multinational Activity, edited by James R. Hines, Jr., 194-199.

Mintz and Smart (2001), "Income Shifting, Investment and Tax Competition: Theory and Evidence from Business Taxation in Canada," *Journal of Public Economics*, 88(6), pp 1149-1168.

Organisation for Economic Cooperation and Development (2005), <u>Model Tax Convention on Income and on Capital</u>. July.

Slemrod, Joel (1990). "The Impact of the Tax Reform Act of 1986 on Foreign Direct Investment to and from the United States," in Joel Slemrod (ed.) <u>Do Taxes Matter? The Impact of the Tax Reform Act of 1986</u>, pp. 168-197.

US Department of the Treasury, Office of Tax Analysis (2002), "Corporate Inversion Transactions: Tax Policy Implications," May.

US Department of the Treasury, Office of Tax Policy (2000), "The Deferral of Income Earned Through U.S. Controlled Foreign Corporations," December.